English Garden Ponds

By Derek Lambert

A Beginner's Guide

Introduction

Water has been an important feature of gardens throughout the ages. Ponds and water features of various types have been found in the gardens of just about every civilization studied by historians. Obviously they have changed over the years depending on what materials have been available to build them and the culture of the people themselves. Running water in the form of small streams or fountains was particularly important in some cultures, whilst others concentrated on creating a more natural looking pond with water lilies and bog plants.

The story of Goldfish as inhabitants of ornamental ponds has its origins in China. The exact date when the first Goldfish was kept has been lost in the mists of time, but ancient Chinese records are said to state the first colored fish were discovered between 265 and 316 A.D. What is known for certain is that they were being widely kept in

What are Quarterlies?

Because having your own garden pond is growing at a rapid pace, information on setting up and stocking such ponds is vitally needed in the marketplace. Books, the usual way information of this sort is transmitted, can be too slow. Sometimes by the time a book is written and published, the material contained therein is a year or two old...and no new material has been added during that time. Only a book in a magazine format can bring breaking stories and current information. A magazine is streamlined in production, so we have adopted certain magazine publishing techniques in the creation of this Quarterlies. Magazines also can be produced much cheaper than books because they are supported by advertising. To combine these assets into a great publication, we issued this Quarterly in both magazine and book format at different prices.

Distributed in the UNITED STATES to the Pet Trade by T.F.H. Publications, Inc., One T.F.H. Plaza, Neptune City, NJ 07753; distributed in the UNITED STATES to the Bookstore and Library Trade by National Book Network, Inc. 4720 Boston Way, Lanham MD 20706; in CANADA to the Pet Trade by H & L Pet Supplies Inc., 27 Kingston Crescent, Kitchener, Ontario N2B 2T6; Rolf C. Hagen Inc., 3225 Sartelon St. Laurent-Montreal Quebec H4R 1E8; in CANADA to the Book Trade by Vanwell Publishing Ltd., 1 Northrup Crescent, St. Catharines, Ontario L2M 6P5 ; in ENGLAND by T.F.H. Publications, PO Box 15, Waterlooville PO7 6BQ; in AUSTRALIA AND THE SOUTH PACIFIC by T.F.H. (Australia), Pty. Ltd., Box 149, Brookvale 2100 N.S.W., Australia; in NEW ZEALAND by Brooklands Aquarium Ltd. 5 McGiven Drive, New Plymouth, RD1 New Zealand; in Japan by T.F.H. Publications, Japan—Jiro Tsuda, 10-12-3 Ohjidai, Sakura, Chiba 285, Japan; in SOUTH AFRICA by Lopis (Pty) Ltd., P.O. Box 39127, Booysens, 2016, Johannesburg, South Africa. Published by T.F.H. Publications, Inc.

MANUFACTURED IN THE
UNITED STATES OF AMERICA
BY T.F.H. PUBLICATIONS, INC.

Quarterly

yearBOOKS,INC.

Dr. Herbert R. Axelrod,
Founder & Chairman

Neal Pronek
Chief Editor
Glen Axelrod
Editor

yearBOOKS and Quarterlies are all photo composed, color separated and designed on Scitex equipment in Neptune, N.J. with the following staff:

DIGITAL PRE-PRESS
Robert Onyrscuk
Jose Reyes
Tom Roberts

COMPUTER ART
Patti Escabi
Sandra Taylor Gale
Candida Moreira
Joanne Muzyka
P. Northrup
Francine Shulman

Advertising Sales
George Campbell
Chief
Amy Manning
Director

©yearBOOKS
1 TFH Plaza
Neptune, N.J. 07753
Completely manufactured in
Neptune, N.J. USA

China as ornamental fish as far back as 800 A.D. when references to them were often included in poetry.

The arrival of Goldfish in Europe is a little more sure; the first recorded import was in 1611 with two others following in 1691 and 1728. By the middle of the 1700s Goldfish keeping had become very popular with the aristocracy and with it came a general interest in ponds and water gardens. The late 1700's and early 1800's saw the development of many of the hardy water lily hybrids. France was the center of this activity and many of the popular varieties kept today were created at this time by Joseph Bory Latour-Marliac and his son-in-law, Maurice Laydecker. Some of these varieties bear those gentlemen's names and are commonly offered for sale by specialist nurseries and garden centers.

This was the beginning of our modern watergardering era. But it was the development of the flexible but sturdy pond liners and prefabricated ponds which has really helped create the tremendous surge in popularity that watergardening is currently enjoying. Before those materials were available most garden ponds had to be made of concrete. These were very difficult to make and often leaked or cracked. Once this

happened it was a nightmare to repair effectively and many people just gave up in despair.

Prefabricated ponds, especially fibreglass ponds, solved all those problems. Now all you needed to do was dig a hole and plop the pond into position. Butyl and other liners were even better because you could choose exactly the size and shape pond you wanted. With care some will last 50 years or more and if you relocate they are relatively easy to dismantle and take with you.

The only other problem to be solved was green water. This had been the bane of pond keepers since the very earliest days of civilization. You can just imagine the poor old Roman complaining about his pond water having turned green. With careful planting and low numbers of fish a balance could be achieved which would keep the water clear, but it rarely is. More often than not the garden pond resembles a murky green stagnant mire rather than the beautiful centerpiece of a garden that it ought to be.

The inclusion of proper filtration helped reduce this problem, but it was finally eradicated by the most unusual of methods. It was found that by passing pond water over a small U.V. lamp the algae which cause green water can be killed and the pond will stay

permanently clear. Finally we can all enjoy the sight of a crystal clear pond in our gardens.

My own interest in ponds and water gardens started when I was only 9 years old. Like most children of that age I did not stop to read up on the subject and learn how to build a pond correctly, but rushed straight into it one Saturday morning whilst my parents were out shopping. My older brother, who should have had more sense, was persuaded to fall in with my plans and we soon had a hole dug in a corner of the garden. Next came something to line it with. Since pocket money did not stretch to a proper liner, a thin sheet of flexible plastic was purchased at the local D.I.Y. store and while we were out we popped into the local pet shop and bought two Goldfish to go into our new pond. The "liner" was put in the hole and our pond filled with the water from the garden hose. Next the fish were added and we stood back to admire our efforts.

An hour later my parents arrived home to find that our newly installed pond leaked and the water level had already dropped dangerously low. My father was an amazingly understanding man who loved all living things (even children whose insatiable interest in animals led to the house's resembling a zoo rather than a home) and instead of telling us off went out and bought a proper fibreglass pond. That evening our two Goldfish were swimming around their new home. Despite the drastic water changes and general upheaval associated with their arrival, both fish lived to ripe old ages and the one I selected even went on to win prizes at fish shows.

Originally my pond was purely a home for fish but later my interest expanded to amphibians and we soon had a breeding colony of frogs in there as well. At the time these were introduced purely for my own interest but nowadays, with so many wetlands and natural ponds being drained for agriculture, the role of garden ponds in maintaining breeding populations of all types of amphibians has become vital to their survival. This was only too vividly brought home to me seven years ago when just after I moved into my present home the natural pond behind our land was filled in by the farmer. Since there was a breeding colony of newts in there, I decided to provide them with a new home in my garden and dug a replacement pond as quickly as possible. Within a few days of its being filled the newts had taken up residence.

The design of this new pond was different from the others I had had because it was aimed at providing a home for amphibians which needed easy access to the water, so a bog garden area was included. Suddenly a whole new range of plants could be kept and the pond and garden flowed smoothly into each other. This mimics nature much more closely than most manmade ponds because a natural pond changes from a pure aquatic habitat in the center to a marshy habitat at the banks and finally dry land.

In this book I have tried to include all the different types of pond which can be created, but the variety is infinite and you may have ideas of your own which I have not mentioned. Be brave and try them out. Ask your neighbors and friends if they have built a pond and have a look at them. Once a year my village holds a summer festival during which some people open their gardens. I was amazed to find many of the gardens contained a pond or water feature of some sort and several of them gave me ideas to try in my own garden. So don't be afraid to ask around; pond keepers and water gardeners the world over like to share their experiences with other people.

Rich Sacher, a genius water garden designer from New Orleans, designs different ponds for different tastes. You can do the same thing. Part of the pleasure of water gardening is that anything which holds water can grow flowers and probably support fish life. Photo by Rich Sacher.

Contents

41. Fish

50. Other Livestock

54. Bog, Floating and Submerged Plants

63. Poolside Planting

Location, Design and Construction

LOCATION

The location of a pond may well determine how successful it will be in the long term. From a purely aesthetic point of view one part of the garden may be far superior to anywhere else, but if this is under trees, falling leaves, pollen and other debris will pollute the water. Some deciduous trees are worse than others in this

the tree is an evergreen it will not cause a problem. Even evergreens shed leaves and, in some cases, these will poison any fish very quickly. Holly and Laurel are particularly troublesome in this respect but there are many others.

Dangerous substances which can fall into a pond and cause problems are sprays and chemicals

Remember to take into consideration your next door neighbours' activities as well as your own.

Another factor to take into consideration when initially planning a pond is the amount of available light. To be at their best, water lilies need about 5 hours of direct sunlight per day. If buildings cast too much shade over the pond, then your lilies will not thrive and in some cases will fail to flower altogether.

In fact the best position for any pond is right out in the open where it will receive the maximum amount of sunlight possible. Very often this will be in the middle of a lawn and will naturally become a focal point of the garden. In some cases, particularly when a formal pond is being built, the patio will be an obvious choice for a pond. In these circumstances try to position it in an area where as much sunlight will reach it as possible.

Two other factors to think about when planning a pond are distances from water and electricity supplies. Ideally you want them close enough to run a normal garden hose from the tap to the pond for filling and topping up. Unless you are planning a balanced

This formal pond with a statue can be found in Geneva, Switzerland. It is dangerous for fishes because of the overhanging trees. Photo by D. Lambert.

respect. The leaves of Willows and Poplars contain harmful substances, all parts of Laburnum trees are *poisonous*, fruit trees of all kinds drop immature and windfall fruits; all of these will severely pollute a pond and may kill the fish.

Do not think because

used for pest control. Many of these are lethal to fish and aquatic life and can only be used well away from a pond. For this reason do not put a pond near your vegetable plot or other area where there are plants which are likely to be sprayed or treated with chemicals.

natural pond with no filtration or fountains, etc. you will need a convenient electricity supply. If one is not already in place you will have to run an underground cable to the pond.

Since the pond is likely to draw people to it on a regular basis a path of some sort is going to be needed. If one already exists it makes sense to locate your pond so that you can make use of it. If not you will have to work this into your plans and take account of how it will look in relation to the total effect.

Another point to remember is the soil. Some gardens have areas which are almost permanently waterlogged. Logically this would appear to be the ideal location for a pond, but in fact totally the opposite is the case. Any hole dug in this area will partly fill with water. A natural pond, I hear you cry! Well maybe—until the summer months when the water ebbs away and the fish and plants are left high and dry. Trying to build a concrete pond in such a location is impossible and using a liner can be disastrous because the pressure of water underneath it will make it lift away. No, this is one location to steer well clear of.

Another location to try to avoid, and for some

gardeners this will be an impossibility, is any area of heavy clay soil. I had the great misfortune of having a garden made up totally of this difficult stuff and it was the bane of my life. Digging a hole for a pond in this type of soil can be a real killer and should not be attempted by anyone less than 100% fit. My present garden has one area of heavy clay but

A natural pond. Note the slope from dry land into the water. This pond should not be too deep or it may be dangerous for humans and animals. Photo by D. Lambert.

the rest is good loamy soil. Needless to say I avoided the clay area when I built my latest pond.

DESIGN

Designing a pond is not as difficult as you may think but it takes a lot of thought to achieve just the effect you want. First of all you are going to have to decide what type of pond you want. The first

question you need to ask yourself is: "Is it going to be a formal or informal pond?" This is very much a personal choice but whichever you decide on, you have to make the decision right at the outset. As a rough guide a formal pond best suits a formal setting. It would look incongruous to place a rectangular formal pond in the center of a riotous

cottage garden but as the centerpiece of a patio or up against a wall it would be in perfect keeping with its surroundings.

Although the size of a pond will in part be dictated by the area available to contain it and the amount of money available to buy the materials needed to make it, it is always worth remembering that big is

A very pretty garden pond in France. The water is beginning to turn green but since there are no fish in the pond, there is no problem at the moment. Photo by Aqua Press, MP & C Piednoir.

A formal pond in Geneva, Switzerland. The fountain and the sculpture add a great deal to the magnificence of this display. Photo by D. Lambert.

subjecting the fish to wide fluctuations of temperature. Algae will also be encouraged to grow and any pollution will soon build up to a dangerous level. The second problem with a shallow pool is that it might freeze solid during the winter. This will obviously kill the fish and many plants will also be harmed.

In the past it was thought an area of the pond should be four feet or even five feet deep to prevent the water from freezing solid. In temperate climates this great depth is not needed and will not be appreciated by aquatic plants or the person digging the pond. In fact a depth of two feet will, in almost all cases, be satisfactory. In particularly severe climates you may be advised to go a little deeper, say three or even three and a half feet in one area, but this is the maximum useful depth you are ever likely to need.

Apart from the overall depth of a pond you will need to consider areas where you can position marginal plants. These like to have their roots in water and their stems mostly above it. Some species will need a few inches of water above their crown while others will only want their roots in waterlogged soil. This

beautiful with ponds. Small ponds are far more likely to be prey to pollution and algae problems than large ponds are. Your fish will also grow bigger and live longer in a large pond. If you intend to keep Koi then

you absolutely must have a large pond for them.

The depth or your pond is also important. Shallow ponds have two great drawbacks. Firstly there is less water volume which means the pond will warm up or cool down quicker,

means creating planting shelves at about 8 inches below the water level. This will allow you to place pots of marginals that like water above their crowns directly on the shelf and others that only want waterlogged roots can be raised to the appropriate

has an area deep enough for the fish and suitable marginal shelves. It may seem ridiculous that some manufacturers would make a prefabricated pond totally unsuited for the job, but they do.

If you are using a liner or concrete then the shape

rarely work well.

Finally, yet most importantly, you need to consider safety. Ponds represent a real danger to children, elderly people, pets and other animals. If your garden is used by young children to play in, then you are going to have

A beautiful water garden located in an English back yard. Photo by Dr. David Ford.

level with bricks.

Once you have decided on the size, depth and location of your new pond you need to work out its shape. If you are using a prefabricated fibreglass pond then the shape will be set for you. Make sure when you buy it that it

will be up to you. The best place to start is by drawing a plan of your garden and then trying different shapes in the area allocated to the pond. Generally try to keep them simple; fussy shapes with little squiggles of pond poking out here and there

to fence in the pond or make it inaccessible to them in some way. A raised pond might be a better alternative in this sort of situation but make sure there is nothing in the garden which can be used by a child as a ladder. To be honest I would be very reluctant to have any type of pond in my garden if I had young children. It may sound paranoid but children have drowned in only a few inches of water, so why take risks?

Elderly people are far less likely to clamber into a raised pond and drown than children are, but it would be very easy for them to miss their footing at the edge of a submerged

by plants to keep people away from the edge and any path can be kept well clear of the water's edge.

The danger a pond presents to animals is real and was brought home to me when three hedgehogs drowned in one of my ponds over a two-week period. These nocturnal animals fell in while trying to drink the water and despite being able to swim could not escape because

current pond the hog garden area allows any animal which fails into the pond an easy escape route and I have never seen anything drown in this one.

Once you have a design, go outside and mark it out on the ground. A hose can be used for this or a thick piece of rope. When you have positioned it, walk well away to see the general effect. Try looking at it from all angles and even check what you can see from an upstairs window. Once you are sure you are happy with the shape, you can work out the materials you are going to need to make it.

CONSTRUCTING A POND

Prefabricated Ponds

This is probably the easiest type of pond to make but there are certain pitfalls which have to be avoided if you are to have a successful pond. When this type of pond first came out, many designs were far too small and shallow to be useful. Marginal shelves were often too high up the sides to give a proper planting depth and some of the shapes were so complicated and closed in that there was little room for a water lily to grow. Nowadays, I am pleased to say, most of these problems can be avoided by choosing a good design but unfortunately the poor

Safety is a big factor in choosing the design and location of your pond. Young children must be taught that ponds are dangerous and they must be careful. The chair should NOT be close to the pond! Photo by Dr. David Ford.

pond and fall over. Likewise people in wheelchairs could easily glide straight into a submerged pond on a patio. Raising the height of the pond by a foot or two in a formal setting will help prevent this kind of accident. An informal pond can be surrounded

of the steep sides. Eventually they became exhausted and drowned. If there had been some marginal plants, their containers would have created a safe haven for the hedgehogs to rest on until the morning, when I would have been able to rescue them. In my

designs are still out there ready to trip up the unwary buyer.

So what should you look for? First of all, overall size. It is so easy to think a pond is huge when it is viewed propped up against a wall. Take a tape measure with you and check the length and width of each pond. With a rectangular pond, multiplying these two figures together you come up with the surface area which should be a minimum of 50 square feet for a pond in which fish are to be housed. Remember to take into account the odd shapes some prefabricated ponds are when working the surface area out. Amphibian and wildlife ponds can be smaller but you will not be able to have any of the larger water lilies in these if they are too small.

Next you need to check the depth. In at least part of the pond this must be 18 inches or better still 2 feet. Finally measure how deep the planting shelves are. They must be about 10 inches down the sides. This allows for the water to be a couple of inches below the edge of the pond and still leaves the deep water marginal plants enough water over the top of them.

The final thing to take into account is the material they are made of. Ideally this should be resin bonded fibreglass. This is very tough but flexible and will last for many years, but this type of pond is more expensive than less durable plastic ponds. For a raised pond you must use fibreglass but for a normal pond, providing you are prepared to replace it a few years down the way, plastic may be satisfactory.

To install a prefabricated pond all you

Almost anything can be turned into a container for growing plants along the edge of the pond. Photo by D. Lambert.

need do is dig a hole slightly larger than the pond. If the pond is to be surrounded by paving stones, then it will need to be positioned 2 inches deeper than the surrounding ground. This allows the stones to be laid level with the soil. Position the pond so it is sitting on a firm base and is level. Use a long piece of wood resting on each side with a spirit level on it to be sure of this. Then carefully fill in the gap all the way around. Make sure you fill the space under each shelf with soil and finally check the level again. You are now ready to fill your new pond.

POND LINERS

These come in several different forms. Originally polythene (polyethylene) was used but even thick grades of this were very susceptible to puncturing. Above the water level the polythene would disintegrate because of ultraviolet rays in sunlight. This meant the effective life of a pool made of polythene was only 12 to 18 months before it had to be replaced.

Nowadays two different materials are used as pond liners. Laminated

P.V.C. (polyvinyl chloride) is the cheapest and works well. It is supposed to have a life of at least 10 to 15 years and many come with a guarantee of this. Just what your local pond supplier would make of a customer returning a pond liner after 8 years I hopefully won't have to replace it in your lifetime. Being so durable also means you can take it with you when you move.

To calculate the size of liner needed for your pond all you have to do is measure the maximum length of the pond and wide by 2 ft deep, will need a liner 12 ft long and l0 ft wide. If you are planning to incorporate a bog garden area as part of your pond then you must include the size of this in your maximum length and width calculations. So if a bog garden area of 2 ft all

Butyl rubber sheeting is the best material for making a plastic-lined water garden. But you have to be neat about it. The edges should be hidden with large stones. The exposed submerged part will quickly turn black with algal growth. Photo by Aqua Press MP & C Piednoir.

don't know but no doubt this will happen somewhere down the line.

In my opinion, far and away the best material for making ponds is butyl rubber sheeting. This is supposed to last for up to l00 years, so although it is more expensive you add twice the maximum depth. This gives you the overall length of liner needed. Width is calculated in the same way, by measuring the maximum width and adding twice the maximum depth. So a pond 8 ft long and 6 ft round the pond is required then the liner must be 16 ft long and 14 ft wide.

Since most liners come in prepackaged sizes you will probably have to work out the maximum pond size you can make from a given size. In this case you have to subtract twice the depth from the length and width of a liner. Hence a 12 ft long by l0 ft wide liner will create a 2 ft deep pond of 8 ft long by 6 ft wide. Once again remember to figure in any bog garden area in the calculations.

hole are in no danger of falling in.

The bog garden area should be dug out last of all. This will need a retaining wall where it joins the main pool, so leave a 4-inch-thick wall and dig out the soil behind this to a depth of 9 inches.

sharp objects. I found over a dozen rusty nails when building one of my ponds, any one of which could have punctured the liner, so be thorough in your search—your pond's life could depend on it.

Next you need to line the hole. A covering of

By having a water input via a fountain, the water becomes aerated and loses some of the chlorine or fluorine it may contain, and it then is tunneled through to the main pond from which it may escape via an overflow pipe. Photo by Dr. David Ford.

To install the liner you must first dig a hole of the appropiate size and shape. Include any marginal shelves and slope the walls outwards slightly. A 20 degree slope is the ideal but this does not have to be very accurate so long as the sides of the

Next lower the wall by 3 inches so that the liner will be below the water surface when the pond is filled.

Once all the digging has been done, carefully scrutinize the bottom and sides of your new pond, removing any stones and

sifted soil will do the job but since this needs to be a couple of inches thick it is often easier to use sand, peat, fine sawdust, several thicknesses of newspapers or better still old carpet or carpet underlayment. The idea is to make a safe surface for your liner to

Below: Building a magnificent garden pond in France starts with a good location, out in the open, with no trees. Photos in this series by Aqua Press MP & C Piednoir.

Below: The form of the pond is dug out of the compacted soil and very rich concrete (3000 psi) is used for the foundation.

The walls are put up next with a lighter cement mix.

rest on. This is most important for the bottom of the pond and any marginal shelves because it is these areas which are likely to have containers resting on them. In most cases you only need to line these areas and can ignore the sides but if you have very stony soil the sides will also have to be covered or at the least very carefully checked for sharp stones. The area around the top of the hole must always be covered.

Now lay your liner over the hole with an equal amount of sheeting hanging over the sides. Carefully place bricks all around the sheet's edges to hold it in place and then start to fill with water. As the water accumulates in the middle it will pull the liner towards the bottom of the hole and stretch it taut. Some of the bricks should be removed to allow the liner to pull into the hole a little more but enough should remain to keep it taut. The water will gradually push the liner onto the sides and stretch it around corners, creating a smooth finish. However, some wrinkles will inevitably form but these can be kept to a minimum by carefully pulling the liner into position as the pond fills. This job is likely to take several hours depending on the size of the pond. In the end the pond will be full and about

6 inches of liner will be left all around the edges.

How you finish the edges will depend to a certain extent on what style of pond you are making. Paving stones can be used all around the pond or for just part of the edges. If these are to be flush with the surrounding garden then you will have to remove 2 inches of soil before cementing the stones on top of the liner. The stones should project for a couple of inches over the edge and can be cemented into place using a mixture of 1 part cement to 3 parts sand. Try to keep this away from the edge as much as possible since if it fails into the water you will have to empty the pond and refill it after the cement has been removed.

For a more natural look you may want grass right up to the edge. To do this fold the liner over and bury it in the soil as close to the pond's edge as possible. Next lay turf around the edge and allow it to hang over the edge and into the water. An alternative to using grass would be to plant miniature prostrate evergreens around the edge. These cover the edges in a natural way and provide hiding places for amphibians.

If a bog garden area has been included fill the pond to only just below the retaining wall. Then fill the

Above: The water supply and overflow pipes are put in while the cement is still soft. *Below:* Insets can be put into the wet cement.

Below: Before the pond is finished, it should be filled with water to aid in the setting of the cement and to be sure there are no leaks. The water cannot be used for plants or fish because it will have been affected by the leaching of the concrete.

A large hole is dug into the middle of the pond as this is where the debris will accumulate and this is where a siphon will be most effective in removing the debris.

bog garden area with sterilized meadow loam and bury the excess liner in the soil. Bank the loam up from the retaining wall to make the bog garden area continuous with the rest of the garden. Now continue to fill the pond so your bog garden is covered with water. Some soil will float away into the main pool but this will soon sink and will do no harm.

CONCRETE PONDS

Originally clay was used to make artificial ponds but these often leaked and required a great deal of skill to make. Generally ornamental ponds were only found in the gardens of the aristocracy and gentry and were well beyond the means and skill of most gardeners. Some lucky individuals had a natural pond in their garden but these were very few and far between. When concrete came along it represented a great step forward and brought the hobby of water gardening into the realms of small garden owners.

Although concrete is rarely used to make ponds now, it still has its uses and some people prefer the more natural texture and appearance of this type of pond. I will, therefore, run through the technique used to make one of these ponds. I would most strongly advise you not to undertake making a concrete pond unless you are perfectly fit and have some D.I.Y. experience with both woodworking and the use of concrete.

Concrete is a very strong but heavy and rigid material. When too much stress is placed upon it, instead of bending it simply cracks. With a concrete pond there are two main causes of cracking: firstly a thick sheet of ice will place great stress on the walls and secondly settlement of the soil underneath the pond puts stress on the base which eventually cracks. Both risks can be minimised when building the pond and with a lot of hard work a very serviceable pond can be created.

The first difference with a concrete pond is in the size of the hole. You need to make it at least 6 inches bigger all around than the size of pond you want to create. The base will need to be 12 inches deeper as well and the walls need to have a 20 degree slope to them. Once this has been dug out you then need to ram the base and sides as firmly as possible. Now put a 6 inch layer of hardcore on the bottom and ram this down.

Your woodworking skills now come to the fore. Since the sides of the pond are very steep you will have to make shuttering to hold the concrete in place

This formal pond and statue came from the ancient city of Pompeii, Italy. It was buried for 2,000 years!!! The workmanship of the tile and edging are breathtaking. Photo by D. Lambert.

while it is setting. This is why concrete ponds are best made in simple shapes such as squares or rectangles. Curves can be created by bending

Heavy plastic liner can be used for a water garden. The edge should be hidden with paving stones, not only to hold the plastic from caving in, but to hide the ugly edge. Photo by Dr. David Ford.

The pond shown being built on the previous pages, after its completion. Photo by Aqua Press MP&C Piednoir.

hardboard into the shape needed and fixing this onto the framework but it can be very tricky. When you have finished you should have a wooden framework which mirrors the shape of the pond with its 20 degree slope to the walls but is 6 inches smaller than the hole. Don't forget to include any marginal shelves when making the shuttering, although these can be added after the main pond has been built but before the sealant is applied.

Once your shuttering is made you can now make your pond. Since it is important to complete the task in a single day it is wise to have everything to hand and make sure you have enough of it. As a rough guide 2 cwt of cement, 2 cwt of sand and 4 cwt of coarse aggregate will produce enough concrete for 20 sq ft of area. You will also need to add a waterproofing powder to the mix. Usually $2^{1}/_{2}$ lb of this will be enough but check the manufacturer's instructions.

When you make up the concrete, mix all the dry ingredients by volume first and then add water until it is a thick paste which will hold its shape when cut by a spade. Mix only what you need at the time and try to use it as soon as possible.

First of all cover the base in a 4 inch thick

This pond, built above the ground, has a window which allows an interesting underwater view. Photo by M P & C Piednoir.

layer of concrete. Then lay a piece of reinforcing mesh or chicken wire on the top and cover it with another 2 inch layer. Leave this for an hour before installing the shuttering. Now pour concrete between the shuttering and the hole. This will form the walls of the pond.

When the concrete is firm enough to stand on (this will usually be a few days but will depend on the weather) the rendering instructions on this. As before all the ingredients need to be mixed dry; then add enough water to turn it into a thick paste. The whole pond is then coated with an inch thick layer of this mixture.

When everything has dried and the pond has leaching out and poisoning fish and plants.

The only problem with this is the risk that if it is damaged the lime will start to leach out with disastrous consequences. The better alternative is to fill the pond with water and leave it for a week.

A very nice raised pond. Note the lion head through which overflow water pours out onto a stone during heavy rains. This pond has a plastic liner which is well hidden under the flagstones. Photo by Dr. David Ford.

coat needs to be applied. This is made from 1 part cement with 3 parts sand and a waterproofing powder usually added at the rate of 5 lb per cwt but once again check the manufacturer's had a chance to harden for a week, a coat of pond sealant can be painted over the concrete. This clear coat seals the concrete behind an impervious barrier, preventing lime from Then scrub around with a wire brush and empty the pond, making sure any sediment is removed. Then refill the pond and leave it for another week before repeating the process. Do this every week for about

two months before checking the pH of water which has been in the pond for a week. This should be similar to the pH of the water with which the pond was filled. If the reading is more than 0. 2 degrees higher than the original water then continue the washing process and check a week after each wash. Once the pH has been stabilized within safe limits you can add plants and a week or two later fish.

BUILDING A RAISED POND

Raised ponds, particularly those on patios or by walls, are best made of cement blocks or bricks. In many ways these are far easier to construct than even butyl rubber liner ponds and in a formal setting are very attractive.

The first thing to sort out is the base. This is made from 1 part cement, 2 parts sand and 3 parts coarse ballast mixed together thoroughly before making into a stiff paste with water. The concrete is then poured into a wooden form of the correct size and allowed to set. Next put a line of mortar along

This series of photographs shows the step-by-step construction of a raised pond. The pond is two leveled. The upper level will eventually be sealed off and used for raising young fry. Photos by Aqua Press M P & C Piednoir.

the edge of the base and start laying the blocks or bricks on this. Use a spirit level to make sure the wall is being laid level and continue to build the pond up to the desired height. Leave to set for a day before adding a 1 inch thick coat of rendering in the same way as for the concrete pond. Once again the pond can either be sealed or go through the washing process as previously described.

DRAINAGE AND OVERFLOWS

Bottom drains can be plumbed into any of the

Piping has to be added to make the pond suitable for fishes and plants. It is already pea green because of the alkalinity generated by the leaching cement. Photos by Aqua Press MP&C Piednoir.

The completed raised pond whose construction was shown on the facing page.

ponds described here but they create an area of potential weakness which may eventually start leaking. In general, it is better to buy a water pump and empty your pond with this instead of taking the risks inherent in trying to create a bottom drain.

Fitting an overflow pipe at the desired water level is not necessary in submerged ponds but might be of use in a raised pond where the surplus water can be piped to a drain. The pipe does not have to be very thick but it is a good idea to protect the end entering the pond with a fine mesh to prevent small fish and debris from being washed down it.

Water Features

FOUNTAINS

Ever since people have been creating gardens, fountains of various types have been included. Originally these relied on water channelled from a source higher than the fountain, so they could only be included where a suitable source was nearby. Today, of course, we have electric pumps to do the same job, so fountains can be included in any pond or even be made water features all on their own.

The Trevi Fountain in Rome is one of the most famous fountains in the world but is not part of a garden at all. In fact it is a very elaborate wall fountain which operates with spring water channelled through an underground aqueduct. Hence the fountain had a twofold purpose of both looking beautiful and providing a source of clean drinking water for the people of the city.

Many garden centers now stock wall fountains and these make an interesting addition to the garden or a formal pool with a wall on one side. They consist of a

Lovely fountains are to be found in hundreds of shapes and sizes. You just have to search them out. Photo by Michael Gilroy.

submersible water pump in the base pool connected by a flexible pipe to a spout usually hidden in the mouth of a gargoyle. This is positioned on the wall at a height of between 3 and 5 ft and the water falls back into the base pool making a pleasant splashing sound. When installing one of these you should hide the pipe behind the wall by drilling holes through it just above the pond's water level and at the height of the outlet.

In a garden, fountains give life and vibrance to a pond which otherwise would be an area of total calm. Personally, I have always steered clear of them for my own ponds simply because they are best suited to a formal setting and my ponds have always tended towards the informal. Italian gardens have traditionally abounded with statues and fountains in very formal settings and today you can still find many lovely examples of these throughout Italy and the continent.

The easiest fountain to create is produced when a jet unit is attached to a water pump. This is normally directed straight up and produces a pleasant effect. Very high jets are best avoided because on a windy day the water can be blown right out of the pond. It is amazing how fast a pond can be emptied this way!

The usual fountain spray is located in the center of the pond so the water is not shot out of the pond. During high winds it is possible for a pond to be almost emptied as the spray is blown out of the pond itself. Photo by Michael Gilroy.

Another factor to remember when positioning your fountain is that water lilies do not like the strong water movement a fountain creates. It is, therefore, a good idea to keep it well clear of any lilies in the pond.

Moving on from this very simple fountain, there are a great number of

Above: This lovely twin fountain is located in Amalfi, Italy where it served for hundreds of years as a drinking place for horses. Photo by D. Lambert. *Below:* One of the world's most treasured fountains is the Trevi Fountain in Rome, Italy. This is a rare wall fountain. Photo by D. Lambert.

commercially produced fountains with multiple jets and colored lights or statues which spout water. The range is huge and the choice is very much a personal one but it is a good idea to ask your family's opinion about which one to buy because they are going to have to live with it as well as you.

Alternatively, you might like to try making your own cobble fountain. This is one of the simplest and easiest water features to install and brings the sound of water movement into almost any location. I think it looks best in a formal setting but you might like to try it in a shady nook in the garden instead. All you need to make it is a small pond liner, some large cobbles, a piece of thin but strong plastic sheeting and a water pump with a jet attachment or a piece of hose depending on the effect you want to create.

First of all dig a hole deep enough to accommodate the water pump and a layer of cobbles on top. This should be large enough to comfortably site the pump and associated pipes in. Then dig the rest of the area out to the depth of your cobbles. If you are going to have a jet fountain

Not like the Italian fountains shown on the facing page, but certainly a lot more affordable. Most pet shops carry this fountain. Photo by Dr. D. Ford.

then you will need an area some 9 ft square for a jet 3 ft high. Smaller jets will need less area and if you use a hose outlet instead of a jet you will only need an area 3 ft square. The hose outlet produces a lovely bubbling up of water similar to a natural spring.

Once the area has been dug out, carefully remove any stones and line the hole with damp newspapers. The pond liner can now be positioned and the pump put in the deeper hole. Next, punch 1 inch holes all over the perspex sheet and cut a hole in the center large enough for the pump's outlet. This sheet is then placed over the pump and rests on the shallower area forming a platform to hold the cobbles above the pump. Now cover the whole area with cobbles so none of the liner can be seen except the surplus around the edges. This can now be trimmed off and the outlet hose cut down to the level of your cobbles. Your new cobble fountain can now be filled with water and switched on.

WATERFALLS

Waterfalls are something of a more recent development and have

Above left: A wall fountain located in the medieval city of Siena in Italy. These fountains served as a central water supply to the citizens of Siena 500 years ago. Photo by D. Lambert.
Above right: A clever use of a rigid clear plastic sheet along which the water cascades without creating excessive turbulence. Photo by Dr. David Ford.

By keeping the fountain running in the wintertime, the water is kept clear of the ice in the area of water impact, thus allowing the water to "breathe". Photo by Dr. David Ford.

gained in popularity in recent years. The idea to include a waterfall probably came about when a gardener was trying to decide what to do with the massive pile of soil created when a pond is dug out. This often ends up as a rockery but can equally well be used as a basis for a small pond which overflows into a waterfall, stream or series of cascades.

In this case the outflow of a water pump is

A many-tiered waterfall keeps the pond well aerated. Photo by Mary E. Sweeney.

attached to a hose which is buried underground and taken to the top pond. It is important to make sure the pump is strong enough to push the water up the pipe. Some cheap pumps can raise water only 1 foot above the lower pond's

The flow of water over a waterfall can be diminished and the water can be more efficiently oxygenated with a series of steps like those shown here. Photo by Mary E. Sweeney.

surface, so if you have a waterfall which starts above this height no water will reach the top.

There are plenty of prefabricated fibreglass watercourses which can be installed in the same way as a pond or you can use butyl liner to create your own. When installing a butyl liner waterfall start at the base pond and work up the watercourse. Be careful to make sure the edges of the watercourse are high enough to contain the flow of water or once again you will be in danger of emptying your pond. For a more natural finish you can cover the liner with a layer of gravel or pebbles and finish off the lip before

a drop with a piece of stone. This only works if the gradient is not too steep or the gravel will slip down the slope and fall into the lower pond.

The edges can be finished with rocks placed over the liner's edge combined with lots of marginal plants. With a little thought and some hard work you can create a natural looking stream and waterfall which will really enhance your pond.

If you are limited in space around your pond, why not try a halfway house between a fountain and a waterfall? Place the water pump where you want the water feature to be in your pond and attach a piece of hose to the outlet so that about 1 foot is

Long drops of the waterfall increase the turbulence and force of the water. The waterfall shown here is too powerful for the ordinary garden pond. Photo by Michael Gilroy.

The force of the water is increased by the narrowing of the aperture through which the water passes. Photo by Michael Gilroy.

OTHER WATER FEATURES

In recent years there has been a surge of interest in small water features containing water, plants, fountains, etc. Most of these are too small for Goldfish to be successfully maintained in them but they add an extra dimension to your garden or patio. There are many different types available ready made from pool supply centers but you can also make your own very simply and cheaply by using half a barrel.

First of all you need to track down half a wooden barrel. Many garden centers sell these as plant containers so you should not have too much trouble obtaining one. This may or may not be watertight so it is a good idea to line it with butyl liner just to be on the safe side. When doing this take great care that no sharp nails or splinters are sticking out and use old carpet or underfelt to line the barrel.

The container can now be filled with water. Before you do this position the barrel in its permanent

This is a clever water garden. The plants are grown in shallow pans which are easily moved. Photo by Dr. David Ford.

showing above the water. Another piece of pipe 2 feet long should be attached to the intake and left loose on the bottom of the pond. Next build an island using large well washed boulders placed around the pump and on top of each other keeping clear of the intake hose and the outlet hose in the center. Smaller pebbles and pots containing marginals can be used to fill in the gaps. The island should be high enough to cover all but the very tip of the hose which can be disguised with smaller pebbles or plants. When the pump is on, water will gush out of the top of the island and create a mini waterfall.

position. If this is not on a paved area, make sure the ground is level and packed down hard. Once in position never attempt to lift a full barrel. Water is remarkably heavy and you will probably do yourself an injury trying to lift this much.

When filling the barrel

This huge pot has a spray running in it to show potential customers that it is waterproof and can be used as a miniature water garden.

keep the liner taut so it stretches into the container's shape and use newspaper to cover the barrel's edges. Once full, the surplus liner can be trimmed off and the newspaper removed from around the edges.

Now you can add marginal plants in containers and, if you like, a small fountain. A few pots of oxygenating plants should also be added if you want to include fish. Good species for inclusion in this kind of setup are *Gambusia affinis* or any of the

Your local garden supply center will usually have garden ornaments. There are dozens of sizes and shapes. Photo by Michael Gilroy.

Mexican goodeids. These cannot be left out during the winter but will eat the mosquito larvae which breed profusely in such a setup during the summer months.

BRIDGES & STEPPINGSTONES

The inclusion of bridges and steppingstones in the water garden has its roots in Oriental gardens which tried to recreate in miniature the countryside

Above: European garden ornaments are available...the best ones are found in Italy! Photo by Michael Gilroy.

Left: This bridge is very efficient, but the green water indicates that there is a serious problem with this pond. Photo by Aqua Press MP&C Piednoir.

An inexpensive bridge that can easily be built. Two views. Photos by Michael Gilroy.

around them. Small bridges would be positioned where they could be viewed from the other side of the pond so the reflection would add to the picture formed. In general these bridges were miniature fakes not used to actually cross the pond itself but in some larger gardens small bridges would be constructed so that the path would cross over a watercourse between ponds. It is perfectly possible to recreate this sort of thing in your own garden providing you make sure it is strong enough to take a person's weight.

Steppingstones are another item which can add to a water garden but if your pond is made with a liner then you will not be able to use them to walk over the pond. This is because your weight plus the stone's sharp edges may puncture the liner. If you have a concrete pond then you can make some steppingstones at the same time you construct the pond and these will be perfectly safe for regular use. It is worth remembering children are drawn to steppingstones like bears to honey. Since one wrong step can lead to a serious accident it is best not to include this feature in a pond frequented by children.

Filtration and Pond Maintenance

FILTRATION & GREEN WATER

Green water has been the bane of pondkeepers' lives since ornamental fish have been kept in ponds. It is caused by free-floating algae which feed on nitrates and phosphates in the water. These are a direct result of waste products produced by fish and other animals in the pond. Phosphates are present in fish feces and are the waste products of the vegetable component in a fish's diet. Nitrates are produced by a more convoluted route. Ammonia in fish urine is broken down by *Nitrosomonas* bacteria, which live in water, into nitrites. Then *Nitrobacter*, which live on any static surface, break the nitrites down into nitrates.

Both ammonia and nitrites are poisonous to fish and to a lesser extent so are phosphates and nitrates. In a natural pond the latter two waste products are taken up by plants and used as a food. The level of ammonia and nitrites is kept low by the action of the bacteria and the fact only a few fish live in a natural pond. This way a balance between growing plants, bacteria and fish is achieved.

Whether you need to include a filter of some sort in your pond will depend very much on what creatures it will house. If the pond is a wildlife pool with no fish in it at all, then you need not worry about filtration. Just have lots of growing aquatic plants and some floating plants or water lilies as well. To start with this sort

Water gardens need filters to help keep them healthy, and there are a variety to choose from. A flat model has the double advantage of increased surface area and suitability of use in shallow water. Photo courtesy of EHEIM.

of pond will turn bright green with algae but after a few months when the plants have become established, the water will clear and should remain so.

If you are just going to have a goldfish pond with maybe a few other fish in it as well, then you can create a balanced environment by keeping the number of fish down to the stocking levels quoted in the section on fish species and including lots of growing aquatic plants. This way filtration will not be essential but your pond will still go through a period of a few months when the water will be pea green and most springs you will experience a recurrence of the algal bloom. This will, however, not harm the fish.

If your pond is basicaily going to be a fish pond with little in the way of aquatic plants you will need some sort of filtration to maintain a healthy environment. Without this the water will turn permanently green and waste products will build up eventually killing the fish. This is especially true if you plan to keep Koi.

Filtration has traditionally fallen into three categories— mechanical, chemical or biological. Today we have a fourth type which does not

When the algae takes over the pond, it becomes what the trade calls "pea soup".

Above and below: There is nothing that ruins the pleasure of a garden pond more than uncontrolled algae. The algae killed almost all of the water lilies. Photos by Aqua Press. MP&C Piednoir.

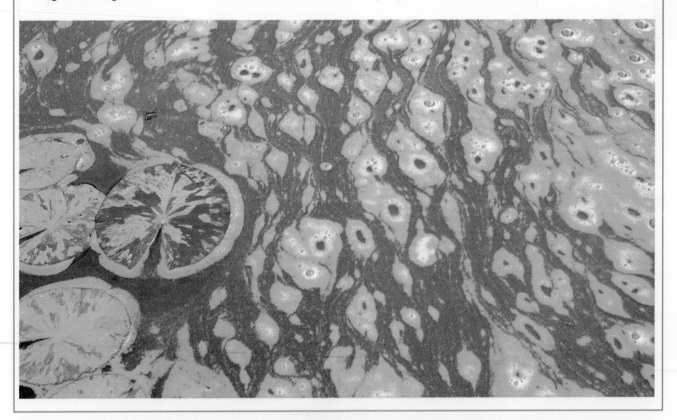

really fall into any of these and probably does not even qualify as filtration. It is in fact more of a form of eradication. This is U.V. filtration (short for ultraviolet light filtration).

Looking at the traditional forms of filtration first:
Mechanical - These filters use some sort of filter medium to catch the solid particles and concentrate them in one place. This helps keep the water clear of mulm and other sediment but has no effect

included in mechnical filters to produce an element of chemical filtration as well. Unfortunately the filter medium needs to be regularly replaced for it to remain active and in a pond situation this sort of filtration is almost worthless.

Biological - This sort of filtration relies on bacteria to break down the waste products, both liquid and solid, and is very commonly used in aquaria today. The

large surface area for the bacteria to live on, whilst water is pumped through it. Others use long brushes or even hair curlers to provide the large surface area needed. In aquaria the gravel substrate is often utilized as a filter medium, with water being drawn through it by a pump. If you have a watercourse between two ponds with gravel covering the liner to recreate a miniature river you will actually have created a biological filter

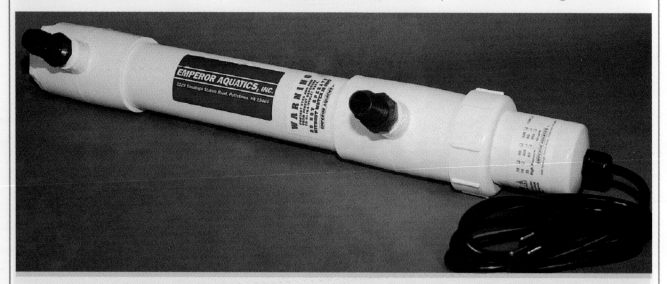

This is simply absolutely necessary for keeping a pond free of all algae! The ultraviolet germicidal energy is superior for killing algae, bacteria and protozoans exposed to its rays. Contact your garden pond supplier or write to Emperor Aquatics, 2229 Sanatoga Station Road, Pottstown, Pa 19464 (phone 610-970-0440).

on algae or soluble wastes such as ammonia. These filters are only effective whilst the filter medium is clean and must be regularly maintained to have any long term value.
Chemical - Chemical filtration works by absorbing the waste products produced by fish into a filter medium. Activated carbon is often

bacteria which do this remarkable job have a few requirements to keep them happy. Firstly they need something to live on and secondly they need oxygenated water flowing over them.

To fulfil these two requirements many different systems have been evolved. Some use special sponges to create a very

bed without realising it.

Whatever design you plump for it will normally be combined with a mechanical prefilter. This means you must regularly clean this section of the filter out or its effectiveness will be reduced.

U.V. Filtration
U.V. filters work by passing water around a

U.V. source which kills algae and bacteria. In strong doses it will also kill many parasites as well and will help reduce the risk of disease in a pond. They are very effective at clearing green water and have been an absolute godsend when it comes to Koi ponds but they do not have any effect on breaking down the waste products fish produce. For this reason they need to be used in conjuction with an effective biological filtration system if the environment is to remain healthy. Many companies now produce combined filters which include mechanical, biological and U.V. elements, thus producing a very efficient filtration package.

MAINTENANCE

On the whole the maintenance your pond will need is very little. A wildlife pond will need periodic top-ups during dry spells and the plants will have to be cut back from time to time to maintain some clear water. Otherwise it can be left very much to its own devices.

Goldfish ponds where you are trying to maintain a balance between fish and plants need more careful watching. Plants must not be allowed to become overgrown and if your fish are successfully breeding in the pond then their numbers must be thinned every year. In the autumn all the dead lily leaves must be removed and any leaves which have blown in from nearby trees must be taken out. At this time of year the oxygenators should be cut back to leave 6 inches of growth above the container's surface.

Fish ponds with filtration must have the filters maintained on a regular basis. Once a week is ideal and it is best if you set aside a specific time and

turns a cloudy grey color then it is being polluted by organic matter of some sort. This may be a dead body or vegetation of some sort which must be found and removed. Immediately change at least half the water in the pond and if possible do the same again a few days later. Unless this situation is corrected early enough all the fish will die.

Cleaning a pond is an annual task. The pond should be stripped bare. The gravel should be washed and the sides should have the algae scraped off. Photo by Dr. David Ford.

day each week to do this. In the autumn any dead leaves must be removed and it is often a good idea to cover your pond with a net at this time of year to make the job easier.

In all ponds lilies and marginals will need dividing and repotting every few years. This is an important chore which will make all the difference in the vigour of the plants in your pond.

If the water in your pond

WINTER ICE

Winter ice is a great worry to many pondkeepers because they fear it will kill their fish. In fact, providing the pond has been dug deep enough, it should not be a problem. What I like to do when my pond freezes over is make a hole in the ice and remove some of the water to produce an air gap between the ice and water. The hole is then covered, thus creating a form of double glazing which helps

Above: Winter arrives. The ice and melting snow could cause some problems unless sufficient drainage is available. Below: Spring is what makes winter bearable! Photo by Dr. David Ford.

prevent the water from freezing any more.

Otherwise the only real threat to fish from ice is the fact it shuts in any gases produced by decaying plant or animal matter. If these build up under the ice, over a period of time they may eventually reach a level where they will kill the fish. Removing any dead plant matter and leaves in the autumn will help prevent this; so will checking the pond every few days during the winter for dead fish or other problems. If a small fountain or other water feature is left running then the pond will not freeze over totally.

Fish

Once your pond has been up and running for a few weeks the time has come to start thinking about obtaining some fish for it. One of the biggest mistakes most pond keepers make is to buy fish from a garden center or aquarium shop and put them straight out in the pond. It is a fact that proper quarantine procedures are not always found in commercial establishments. The best you can normally hope for is that the fish have had a chance to become acclimatised to the water conditions at the shop.

This means you MUST quarantine all new fish you buy before putting them in your pond. I learnt this the hard way many years ago. I bought a very nice healthy looking Pearlscale Goldfish from an aquarium shop with a good reputation and put it straight in with my other fish. About a week later the new fish developed a disease which seemed to be a combination of a parasitic infestation like white spot, a bacterial infection and fungus. Despite advice from a vet and various treatments all the fish succumbed to this disease. If I had quarantined the new fish in a separate tank for a few weeks, then I would only have lost the one fish instead of all of them.

Talking to other experienced aquarists and pond keepers around the world, almost every one has had a similar experience. The diseases differ each time but the effect is always the same. So I beg you to

In conjunction with a quarantine procedure, careful selection of your initial stock will help cut down on problems later. Make sure you take a really close look at any fish you buy. Check there are no open wounds on the body and the fins are held erect.

This crystal clear indoor pond was built by Huang Jinyin, who owns the Rainbow Aquarium Center in Singapore. Photo courtesy of Zen Nippon.

learn by our mistakes and quarantine all new fish for at least two weeks in an aquarium. This allows you to see any problems before they become too serious and hopefully cure the disease before it enters your pond.

If there are a few splits in the fins this is probably nothing to worry about but if they go all the way down to where the fin joins the body or show any cotton wool-like growths on them, choose another. Something to look for is small white spots on the body and fins. This may be a contagious parasite which will need treatment. If even one fish in the tank has this sort of problem do not buy any fish from it.

The quarantine period will allow the new plants to root themselves and settle in and the water to lose any dissolved chlorine gas before fish are introduced. During this time you should have the filter running in the pond so that the bacteria which most filters rely on will have a chance to grow and mature. Unless a U.V. filter is included your pond water will probably turn green with suspended algae. This can be a problem for the fish but once the higher plants have had a chance to become established the water will normally clear.

When introducing fish to a pond, be careful not to just net them out of the quarantine tank and dump them straight in. The water temperature in an aquarium may be very different from your pond and the shock of the change could well harm the fish. Instead float them on the pond in a bucket for 10 minutes and then pour about 25% of the water out and refill with pond water. Leave the bucket for another 10 minutes and tip

A lovely outdoor pond like this is only possible in the summers of temperate zones, or permanently in the tropics. This lovely pond is owned by Peter Loy in Singapore. Photo courtesy of Zen Nippon Airinkai.

a further 25% of the water out and refill. Do this a couple more times and then slowly tip all the water and fish gently into the pond. This way the fish will gently become accustomed to the pond water. A word of warning here about cats and other predators. Keep a close watch on the bucket whilst it is floating on the pond to make sure no cat sneaks up and hooks one of the fish out.

There are many different species of fish which could be included in a pond. Some, like the Goldfish, are so well known that they need no introduction, but others which could be included to good effect are often totally overlooked by the pondkeeper. Some of these are rarely offered for sale and will take a little hunting around to secure. The maximum stocking level quoted in square feet per fish is the amount of surface area needed for each fish of that type. So if you have a pond 10 ft by 10 ft it has 100 sq ft of surface area; therefore you can keep a maximum of 20 Goldfish in a pond this size. The inclusion of two Tench would reduce this to 18 Goldfish, but placing two Koi in the pond instead of tne Tench would leave only enough room for l0 Goldfish.

COMMON CARP

This is really a food fish and was commonly kept throughout Europe in ponds and moats as an additional protein source. Since they grow to a huge size (they can reach l00 lbs in weight when full grown) and are a dull brown color when viewed from above, they do not make very good subjects for the garden pond. In addition to their large size they also have a habit of rooting amongst the plants and eating them. This species can tolerate high levels of pollution and will often survive in conditions where no other

Some goldfish are very close in coloration to the wild carp.

fish could live.

Maximum Stocking Level = 25 sq ft of surface area per fish.

CATFISH

There are a number of species of catfish which would be perfectly suitable for the garden pond, but those species which are most commonly offered for sale are either too large or predators. In Europe you may well come across Wels Catfish being offered for sale, these can grow to 15 ft long and are active predators which will eat all the other fish in a pond. In America you are more likely

This is a Siberian catfish, *Pelteobagrus brashnikowi*. It is a survivor in most garden ponds.

to come across Channel Catfish but these can also be found for sale in Europe as well. These can grow to 3 feet long and have large mouths with which they suck up any unsuspecting fish. Avoid both of these species if you see them for sale and since fish are sometimes mis-named it is wise to give all catfish a wide berth when buying fish for your pond.

GOLDFISH

Goldfish are the most popular pet in the world and are considered by most people as an absolute must for a garden pond. Over the centuries many different

This lovely red and white Ryukin goldfish is too delicate for the usual outdoor pond and is really an aquarium fish. But this hasn't stopped many people from putting it in their outdoor ponds. Photo by Fred Rosenzweig.

types have been bred but not all of them are really suitable for an outdoor pond except in mild climates. The following varieties should all be hardy enough to survive the winter: - Common Goldfish, Shubunkins, Comets and if you can find them Wakin and Jikin

body shape to the Common Goldfish but with two tails instead of one. They come in all colors and are now slowly making their way into the hobby in the U.K. and U.S.A..

Goldfish types to avoid if you plan to overwinter them in the pond are all the short-bodied twintails. You

The common goldfish, usually sold very cheaply as "feeder goldfish" (to be fed to larger fish), makes a good addition to your garden pond. Photo by Michael Gilroy.

A beautiful Pearlscale Goldfish. Not suitable for the usual garden pond. Photo by Fred Rosenzweig.

A Pearlscale goldfish is not a good candidate for the outdoor pond. Photo by Burkhard Kahl.

going to have to set up an aquarium for them during the winter. If this is in an outbuilding it must be prevented from freezing over but otherwise will not need heating.

Maximum Stocking Level

This is a magnificent Black Moor Goldfish. Not suitable for the usual garden pond. Photo by Fred Rosenzweig.

Goldfish. The last two, despite being very old varieties which were developed hundreds of years ago, have never really been commonly available outside of Japan and China. Both have a similar

may be lucky and be able to keep Fantails outside but even these are borderline on hardy. Black Moors and the such like are definitely out of the question. If you really want these types then you are

A single-tailed Red Comet Goldfish. This is suitable for ponds and aquariums. Photo by Fred Rosenzweig.

= 5 sq ft of surface area per fish.

KOI

Koi are becoming increasingly popular because of the wide range of colors they come in, but many people make the mistake of thinking they can be treated in the same way as Goldfish. In fact they grow much larger than Goldfish and do so in a relatively short space of time. They are constantly hungry and will consume great quantities of food which in turn produces huge amounts of waste. In addition they love nothing better than to gobble up any aquatic plants put in the pond so trying to establish a balance between fish and plants is impossible. Good filtration is therefore a must and the larger your pond is the better. Using a U.V. filter is probably the only way you are going to keep the water clear in this kind of pond.

Maximum Stocking Level = 25 sq ft of surface area per fish.

Above: Food designed specifically for feeding koi in ponds are widely available in pet shops and tropical fish specialty stores. In addition to being available in different formulations they also are available in a wide range of container sizes. Photo courtesy of Ocean Star International.

Left: The five-colored Koi called a Goshiki. Photo courtesy of Zen Nippon Airinkai.

A magnificent Ai-goromo Koi. Photo courtesy of Zen Nippon Airinkai.

ORFE

Orfe come in two color varieties, Silver and Gold. It is the golden form which is the more commonly seen in aquatic outlets but both make excellent pond fish. They grow to about 30 inches so are sizable fish and to be kept in the best of health they need some sort of water movement in the pond. Fountains or a waterfall work admirably well in this respect and the Orfe will be seen playing in the current like a school of Dolphins.

Unlike Goldfish and Koi which are omnivores, Orfe

The Golden Orfe, *Leuciscus idus*. Photo by Burkhard Kahl.

are primarily insectivores and will be seen jumping clean out of the water to catch flies as they skim across the surface of the pond. In general a hungry Orfe will eat commercial Goldfish food but it is a good idea to include several feeds a week of carnivore flake food to bump up the protein content of their diet. The Goldfish seem to enjoy the change as well and in the breeding season this extra protein will help in the production of eggs.

When the pond is crystal clear and the fish are trained to come for food, this is what feeding time looks like! Photo by Dr. Herbert R. Axelrod.

Maximum Stocking Level
= 8 sq ft of surface area per
fish.

RUDD

This is a rarely seen fish
which is ideal for medium
to large sized pools. They
grow to about 12 inches
long and have red fins. The
golden form has brighter
red fins and a bronze

The Rudd, *Scardineus erythrophthalmus.*

colored body. All in all a
very attractive fish.

They normally live in
slow-moving streams or
large ponds and lakes
where they can be seen
gliding about just under
the surface. In nature they
feed on small insects and
bits of plants floating on
the top and have difficulty
feeding from the bottom.
They soon adapt to eating
commercial flake and
pellet foods and may live
ten years or more in
captivity.

Maximum stocking level
= 5 sq ft of surface area per
fish.

TENCH

Whilst Goldfish will grub
around the bottom of a
pond looking for food, they
are not as efficient
scavengers as Tench. These
large green fish are peaceful
and unassuming bottom
dwellers which spend all
their lives searching
through the substrate for
food. When young they will
also feed on algae and may
help reduce the growth of
blanket weed.
Unfortunately they are
rarely offered for sale in
aquatic outlets. This is a
real pity because many
ponds would benefit from
the attention of such a
scavenger. Although it
grows to 2 feet it never
becomes a threat to small
fish.

Maximum Stocking Level
= 5 sq ft of surface area per
fish.

FEEDING YOUR FISH

During much of the year
your fish will need feeding

**Tench grows to about 14 inches
in a pond; in the wild they may
reach over two feet in length.**

once a day with a
commercial fish food. Foods
come in a wide variety of
types having been tailored
to the specific needs of
particular fish and have
higher or lower levels of
protein and other
nutriments to keep each
type healthy.

When feeding your fish
only put in the pond what
you can see the fish eat in
5 minutes. If there is
surplus left over after this
time net it out and throw it
away. This will prevent the
pond from becoming
polluted. The only
exception to this is the food
you put in for your Tench.
These are strictly bottom
feeders so enough food
must fall to the bottom of
the pond for them to eat.
For this reason steer clear
of floating pellet type foods
which do not sink quickly.
These are a surefire way to
starve your tench to death.

Many pondkeepers worry
about their fish when they
go away on holiday during
the summer. When I first
asked about this at my
local fish club many years
ago, I was told not to trust

"Hey!! I'm hungry!" This koi sticks his head out of the water to be hand fed. Photo by Michael Gilroy.

Koi are normally bottom feeders but they quickly learn how to take food from the surface. Photo by Michael Gilroy.

Other Livestock

AMPHIBIANS

Village ponds are home to a wide range of wildlife and have traditionally been an important part of any community. Unfortunately many of these village ponds have been drained and replaced by houses and shops in recent times. This, together with the draining of wetlands and many other natural ponds found on farms throughout the countryside, has led to a dramatic failure in the number of amphibians. At one stage extinction for many species was a very great possibility. All this changed with the explosion in water gardening. Suddenly many new habitats are being created in gardens all over the world and amphibians are moving in whenever they can.

Now frogs, toads, newts and salamanders may not be the most attractive of animals to you and you may not care too much about helping save them from extinction if truth be told, but if you love a beautiful garden then they are one of your best allies because they eat huge numbers of slugs, snails and other pests. So everybody has a vested interest in encouraging them into their ponds.

To make a garden pond a haven for amphibians all

A nice addition to a garden pond is a *Triturus vulgaris*. Photo by R.D.Bartlett.

you need do is create a path into and out of the water. The best way to do this is by including a bog garden area with your pond. This produces a gradual change from a purely aquatic habitat to a completely terrestrial one. Thick plant growth, both in the water and surrounding the pond, also helps create habitats for amphibians. A shrubbery or rock garden close to the pond gives hibernating creatures many places to hide. Most species of fish will live happily with amphibians

The Marbled Newt, *Triturus marmoratus*, a female. Photo by Paul Freed.

any non fishkeeper to look after my fish whilst I was away. This advice I am happy to pass on to you. It is far better to leave the fish unfed for two or even three weeks than risk a well meaning neighbour's overfeeding them and polluting the pond, killing all the fish.

In the autumn when the temperature starts to fall your fish will become more sluggish and lose their appetite. When you see this happening reduce the amount of food you are putting in the pond and stop feeding the fish altogether when frosts are regularly occurring at night. By this time your fish will be in hibernation and any food put in the pond will fall to the bottom and rot.
In the spring as the water warms up, your fish will become more active. This is the time when you need to start feeding them again. Take care not to overdo the food at this stage. Stand and watch them eat at first; if they are not really interested in food don't feed them for a few more days.

but they prey on amphibian young, so if you really want to set up a breeding colony you will have to leave the pond without fish or create a small breeding pond separate from your fish pond.

In country areas newts and salamanders will often take up residence in and near a pond all by themselves. My latest pond was dug when the farmer behind our property filled in a natural pond with a breeding colony of newts in it. Those that survived moved over to our new pond within a week and have been breeding there ever since. If your area does not have any newts already or you live in a city then you will have to find someone else who already has a breeding colony and ask for a few for your pond. A couple of pairs is all you need.

Frogs and toads are another matter. The European species tend to return to the pond where they grew up to breed every year. So the introduction of a few pairs of adults to your pond will not work. Instead what you need to do is obtain some frog and toad spawn from a friend who has them breeding in their pond and place this in your pond. Once the tadpoles have grown up they will hop away to forage for food, only

returning to the pond to breed in about 3 years' time when they are sexually mature. In the meantime it is a good idea to add more spawn each year until your first pairs return. Life is tough out there and only a few tadpoles live long enough to reach maturity and return home. So you may find only one makes it back from the first batch or the few that do are all males. Next year's lot may have been more lucky.

The frog *Rana perezi*. Photo by Aqua Press MP&C Piednoir.

Hyla meridionalis. Photo by Aqua Press MP&C Piednoir.

Above: A diving beetle,*Graphoderus.* Photo by Lothar Wischnath.
Below: The water tiger beetle. Photo by Dieter Untergasser.

INSECTS

A pond will attract lots of insects, many of which are useful additions to the ecosystem but others which are downright pests. The primary one which falls into the latter category is the Great Diving Beetle (*Dytiscus marginalis*). This beetle grows to nearly 2 inches in length and has a black body with a yellowish edge. The larva has a much more slender light brown body with feathery breathing tubes on its tail. Both adult and larval forms feed on a variety of soft bodied animals which include fish even much larger than themselves. They do this by holding on to their prey with their claws and sucking the body juices out. If you find a dead fish which has a couple of small puncture wounds then it was almost certainly the victim of this predator. Eradication is relatively easy in a small garden pond because they must come to the surface and breathe from time to time. When this happens all you have to do is net them out.

Just about all the other insects which will visit or take up residence in your pond are not going to be a problem to reasonable sized fish and can safely be ignored. If you are trying to breed large numbers of fish, Water Boatmen and various dragonfly larvae will have to be excluded from the rearing pond because they will eat some of the fry.

SNAILS

Whoever first suggested introducing these pests into aquatic environments, either ponds or aquaria, as "scavengers" has a lot to answer for. Every species of snail I have ever come across feeds on plant life. Some will eat leftover fish food and dead fish as well, so helping reduce the risk of pollution, but good pond management prevents these becoming a problem

One of the many pond snails. *Limnaea.*

anyway. The rest of the time the snails will be munching away at your water lily leaves and aquatic plants. Some authors suggest that certain species only feed on algae and will not harm the plants. Bunkum! From my own personal experience of actually watching these snails feed in an aquarium all the species suggested as doing this also eat new growth of aquatic plants and at a pinch will munch

on lily leaves as well.

Having decided not to have snails in a pond is one thing but keeping them out is something else entirely. The adults can be excluded by soaking all new aquatic plants in a salt bath for a few minutes. This is made using 1 tablespoon of cooking salt per pint of water and will cause the snails to retract inside their shell. A vigorous shake in fresh water will dislodge any

snails still attached to the plants and clean off the salt water. Even doing this with all plants entering the pond does not give you 100% protection from snails. Most snails reproduce by laying clear jelly-like egg masses on plant leaves. These can be very difficult to see but must be removed from all new plants before they are introduced to the pond otherwise you will soon have a snail explosion.

The Water Boatman, *Corixa.* **Photo by Lothar Wischnath.**

Bog, Floating and Submerged Plants

Any pond will benefit from the addition of plants. In many ways they are the real stars of a pond, being both beautiful to look at and having a beneficial effect on water quality. In ponds without filtration you should try to grow as many oxygenating plants as possible because these feed on the same nutriments as algae and will starve this pest out. A good covering of water lily leaves will also help by reducing the amount of light reaching the water.

The following is a selection of commonly found plants but over the last few years the variety of bog plants available has been expanding at a tremendous rate and you may well find many others not listed here. It is always worth checking the trays of perennials as well as the bog garden section in any garden pond center since

Acorus pusillus.

some plants will be found in both sections and they are often sold at a cheaper price as a perennial. When quoted the planting depth refers to the level of water above the plant's crown or soil.

BOG PLANTS

Acorus gramineus - Japanese Rush

There are a number of different rushes which are offered for sale. Many are rather unattractive invasive weeds which when grown in a bog garden will take over and swamp the other plants. The variegated form of this species is semi-evergreen and has pleasant cream-striped leaves which reach 12 inches long. It needs a planting depth of 0–3 inches and is not particularly invasive.

Acorus calamus 'Variegatus' - Sweet Flag or Myrtle Flag

This is a larger broader leafed semi-evergreen rush that has particularly nice leaf color which is flushed pink in the spring. It grows to 30 inches tall and needs a planting depth of 0–3 inches. One of the best rushes for the garden pond.

Alisma plantago- aquatica - Water Plantain

Another particularly invasive plant which made its way into my pond all by

Houttuyni acordata.

itself. It has interesting rounded leaves on long stems which stand up above the water's surface. In midsummer tail spires of tiny write or pinkish flowers appear. These must be dead headed before the seed has a chance to ripen or your pond will be full of this plant next year. Planting depth is up to 12 inches but mine float free in the water which is how they originally appeared.

Butomus umbellatus - Flowering Rush

The Flowering Rush is one plant that really deserves to be planted in every garden pond. It has 3 ft tall grasslike leaves and produces umbels of pink to reddish flowers in the late summer. Planting depth is 3 to 5 inches and the root stock should be divided every few years to ensure prolific flowering.

Caltha palustris - **Marsh Marigold**

One of the best early flowering marginals which is both hardy and adaptable. The species grows to about 2 feet tall with a spread of 18 inches and has single buttercup shaped flowers from March to May. The variety 'Flore Pieno' is more compact, reaching only about 10 inches in height and spread, and is covered with fully double flowers.

Houttuynia cordata **'chameleon'**

This is a wonderful low growing marginal which has basically green leaves splashed with red and yellow. The ideal color is strongest when grown in full sun and whilst it will tolerate water to a depth of 2 inches over its crown it is best grown in moist soil. This is one species which is often found in the perennial section of garden centers.

Iris laevigata - **Water Iris**

Both the original species and the many varieties which have been developed from it are excellent marginal plants for the garden pond. They provide a beautiful show of flowers throughout June and range in color from blue through to white. They grow to 2 $^1/_2$ feet tall and need a planting depth of up to 4 inches. The variety 'Rose Queen' has pink flowers and is probably a hybrid

The purple Irises make a great difference in the color scheme of a garden pond. Photo by Aqua Press MP&C Piednoir.

which would explain why it prefers to have its roots only just covered with water.

Iris pseudacorus - **Common Flag Iris**

This vigorous yellow-flowered iris grows to 3 feet tall and may be invasive if not controlled. The planting depth can be from 0–12 inches.

Lobelia cardinalis - **Red Lobelia**

This lovely plant is

usually sold as a perennial and is only just hardy in the U.K. It does, however, do very well as a marginal plant where its foliage and bright red flowers create a splash of color throughout the summer months. It often overwinters successfully when its crown is covered with 6 inches of water but even if you lose the original plant if it is left to go to seed, lots of seedlings will be produced in the spring. Planting depth 0–6 inches.

Lysichitum americanum - Yellow Skunk Cabbage

This plant is rarely seen in the U.K. but deserves more recognition. In April before the leaves are showing 2-foot-tall bright yellow spathes are produced. This plant loves deep acidic soil and can be grown as a marginal with up to 2 inches of water over the crown or better still in boggy soil by the side of the pond.

Mentha aquatica - Water Mint

The Water Mint has many of the same characteristics of its land cousin, being incredibly invasive. As any gardener who has planted mint in the garden will tell you it never confines itself to the area it was originally planted and will become as much of a weed as dandelions are if given the chance. Even so, it has a lovely scent and produces lilac colored flowers in summer. Its maximum height is 2 $^1/_2$ feet and it needs a planting depth of 0–4 inches.

Myosotis palustris - Water Forget-me-not

Of all the marginal plants I have ever grown this is my absolute favourite. It is a very untidy grower which sprawls around the edge of a pond. During the early summer it produces a prolific display of Forget-me-not-like blue flowers which smother the plant and are really eye catching. It never grows taller than about 6 inches but spreads over a wide area. It prefers a planting depth of between 0 and 4 inches.

Scirpus zebrinus - Porcupine Quill or Zebra Rush

Despite the fact this plant has been available for a long time I only saw it in real life the other day and was really impressed by it. The foliage grows to 4 feet tall and each leaf is circular in section like a porcupine quill and banded with green and white. It likes a planting depth of from 2 to 4 inches and any green stems which appear should be cut out.

Zantedeschia aethiopeca - Arum Lily

Another of my favourite marginal plants, the Arum Lily is hardy in the south of England where it will only survive the winter when the crown is kept under at least 6 inches of water.

In other areas you will need to give it winter protection. The leaves grow up to 3 feet long, are arrow shaped and glossy green. It produces white flowers during late summer which are up to 8 inches long with a central yellow spadix. Plant between 6 and 12 inches deep.

FLOATING PLANTS

Azolla caroliniana - Fairy Moss

Fairy Moss is a charming tiny floating plant which is commonly offered for sale. The fernlike leaves are bright green when the plant is growing in the shade and when the leaves are young but in full sun or as autumn approaches they turn a rusty red color. The only problem with this plant is that it can soon cover the entire surface of a pond, blocking out all the light from the plants below.

For this reason it has to be kept in check by scooping most of it from the surface of the pond every 4 to 6 weeks during the growing season. In autumn remove as much of

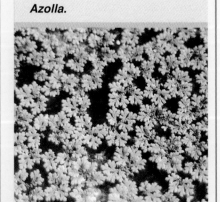

Azolla.

the plant as possible because as it dies back the roots drop off and fall to the bottom, causing a thick sludge to build up. This will rot during the winter and will pollute the water.

Eichhornia crassipes - Water Hyacinth

This plant has been introduced to many tropical areas of the world and is causing great harm to natural habitats. The reason for this is its rapid growth and invasive nature. I have seen miles upon miles of river covered by this plant which blocks out all the light from the submerged aquatic plants, killing them and reducing the oxygen content of the water to such a dangerously low level most of the fish die as well.

All this having been said it is a lovely plant for a

Eichhornia crassipes, the Water Hyacinth.

garden pond. The glossy green trumpet shaped leaves are topped by mauvish blue flower spikes during the summer. Since it is a tender species it is usually grown as an annual with new plants being purchased every year. It is possible to over-winter them on a tank of water in a frost-free greenhouse or conservatory but they rarely survive when kept on the surface of a tank indoors.

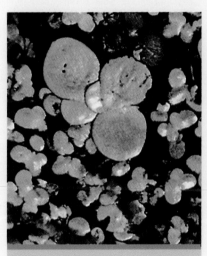

The floating plant Lemna minor.

Lemna sp. - Duckweed

There are several different species of this plant which will happily take over the entire surface of your pond. So invasive and problematic to eradicate is this plant that it is very often considered to be strictly a pest to steer clear of. Once a few floating leaves make their way into your pond they will reproduce at a prodigious rate and soon blanket the surface with a

Water Lettuce, Pistia stratiotes.

thick layer of tiny leaves. Only constant removal will keep some of the surface clear. It is far better not to introduce this pest in the first place. This is one good reason for washing all new plants carefully before introducing them to your pond.

Pistia stratiotes - Water Lettuce

Water Lettuce is similar in many respects to Water Hyacinth and can be just as much of a problem in tropical climates. The leaves look very much like a young lettuce and are a pale green color. They are covered in fine hairs giving them a velvety appearance. Unlike Water Hyacinth it does not have conspicuous flowers but the long feathery roots make a good refuge for fish fry. It must be overwintered in a frost-free environment and all the plants removed from an outdoor pond's surface before the first frost destroys them.

Stratiotes aloides - **Water Soldier**

Another free-floating plant which tends to sit just under or partly above the water's surface. The dense rosettes of leaves are dagger-like and serrated. The flowers are white and rather small but continue in succession throughout much of the summer.

SUBMERGED PLANTS

Aponogeton distachyos - **Water Hawthorn**

Water Hawthorn should be planted in a tub in much the same way as a water lily with just the crown showing above the gravel. It produces small oblong leaves which float on the water's surface and white flowers which are beautifully scented with vanilla. It starts flowering in late spring and continues until the first frost. A lovely rarely seen plant which is well worth including in a pond.

Ceratophyllum demersum - **Hornwort**

Hornwort is an unusual plant in that it does not root itself in the substrate but tends to float in a large mass under the surface. The brittle stems have whorls of bristly leaves which become denser towards the end. It is a good plant for a shaded area in the pond and is easy to establish by just dropping in a clump of the plant. Any lead weight

should be removed before this is done.

Elodea canadensis - **Canadian Pondweed**

This is a very strong robust plant which is often sold by garden pond suppliers as bunches of "Oxygenating Plant". The commonest mistake people make with this plant is to just drop the bunches directly in the pond. What you need to do to grow Canadian Pondweed is open up the lead weight and release the stems. The damaged ends should now be cut off and each piece planted into a pot containing sterilised loam. Place about 4 pieces in a 4" pot. Next cover the soil with washed gravel and carefully lower the pot into position in the pond. Within a few weeks each stem will have taken root and started growing side shoots.

Because this is such a vigorous plant it is a good idea to always keep it confined to pots rather than planting it directly into the substrate where it will have an unrestrained root run.

Myriophyllum aquaticum- **Parrot's Feather**

This is another very good oxygenator which has the added bonus of having part of the plant showing above the water. Each stem is covered with leaves made up of a central stem with tiny side shoots which gives the whole thing the

appearance of a bird's feather.

Once again it tends to be sold in bunches which need dividing up and planting in the same way as Canadian Pondweed. Once the plant stem reaches the surface it continues to grow right out of the water and show off the light green feathery leaves. A lovely plant and a worthy addition to any pond.

Potamogeton crispus - **Curled Pondweed**

This plant is less likely to be found in garden pond centers than the other submerged oxygenators but does an excellent job and looks very attractive as well. The bronze green leaves are thin and wrinkled which makes the plant look a little like seaweed. During the summer months small spikes of tiny red flowers are produced above the water's surface.

When you do find this plant for sale it is usually sold in bunches which should be treated in the same way as described for Canadian Pondweed.

Nymphaea sp. - **water lilies**

There is a huge range of these available ranging in size from pygmy types which only require a planting depth of 8 inches and have a spread of 18 inches to the most vigorous types which need a planting depth of at least

(From left to right) *Rotala macrandra, Rotala rotundifolia, Ludwigia repens, Ludwigia arcuata, Myriophyllum aquaticum* and *Myriophyllum matogrossense.* Drawings courtesy of Holger Windelov.

(Clockwise, starting upper left) The floating *Limnobium laevigatum, Limnobium spongia,* **the large plant known as** *Otellia alismoides, Elodea canadensis, Hydrilla verticillata, Lagarosiphon muscoides* **and** *Egeria densa.*

Above: **The water lily *Nymphaea* c. perfecta. Photo by D. Lambert.**
Below: **A water garden filled with *Nymphaea* Jean Laydecker. Photo by Aqua Press MP&C Piednoir.**

15 inches but prefer 36 inches and have a spread in excess of it. Flower colors come in all shades of red through pink and white with yellow available as well. Some of the tropical lilies have blue flowers which may eventually be hybridised with some of the hardy types to create a blue hardy lily.

When selecting varieties for your pond bear in mind the size and depth of your pond. If you only have a small pond then placing one of the very vigorous varieties in it would soon become a big mistake. This is because the lily will totally cover the pond's surface with leaves which will prevent any light reaching the submerged oxygenating plants, causing them to die back. In a small pond you are, therefore, much better off with smaller less vigorous lilies but these tend to be more difficult to propagate and are more expensive to buy.

Water lilies can be bought either bare rooted or container grown and are best purchased in the early spring when they are stlll dormant. Even if it has been container grown it is best to repot a new lily before placing it in the pond. This gives you a chance to check the health of the tuber and make sure the plant will not need repotting for 3 years.

The size of the container will depend on the vigour of

the lily concerned. Small types will only need a basket 8 inches square, whilst the most vigorous will need an 18 inch basket. Most types, however, are happy in a 1 ft. basket. This should be filled with a good quality sterilised loam or with prepackaged soil sold specifically for pond use.

Water lilies have two distinct types of rootstock. One sort has horizontal rhizomes which grow just below the soil's surface. These must be planted flat about an inch under the soil with just the growing top showing above. The other sort grows vertically and should be planted this way with only the crown showing. Once in position firm the soil well down and cover it with a 1 inch layer of well washed aquarium gravel. Water it using a watering can and then position in the pond.

You will often be told it is necessary to stand a new water lily on bricks to raise it closer to the surface. Then as the plant grows it can be lowered down to its final position in stages. This is supposed to allow the leaves of young water lilies to reach the surface quickly and produce food for the plant, helping it to become established. Later when the plant has grown strong new leaves the basket can be lowered to its final depth. Personally, I think this is a total waste of time and effort, since the

Above: The new water lily called *nigel*. Photo by Aqua Press MP&C Piednoir. Below: The water lily called *Charles de Meurville*. Photo by Aqua Press MP&C Piednoir.

This series of photos shows the steps in planting a water lily tuber. Photos by MP&C Piednoir.

Nymphaea "Conqueror." Photo by Dick Mills.

The water lily called *N. odorata* "Sulphurea Grandiflora." Photo by Dick Mills.

The water lily called Paul Hariot, 190. Photo by Dick Mills.

rootstock will contain all the nutriments needed for the plant to grow leaf stems long enough to reach the surface. I have always put my lilies in their final position at the outset and had a virtual 100% success rate with them. If the stock you originally buy is of good quality then your lily will adapt to its new home very quickly. The only exception to this is seedlings. These must be grown in shallow water for a year before being moved to deeper conditions.

After about three years all the more vigorous water lilies and most of the medium varieties will need dividing and repotting. The best time to do this is late spring to early summer. Lift the container out of the water and remove the water lily from it. Wash off the rootstock and using a sharp strong knife cut off pieces of outer rootstock growth. These should be about 6 inches long and have a growing point or eye. Each of these pieces can then be potted up in its own container and labeled with the variety name if it is known. They can then be returned to the pond.

The following is a list of well known hardy varieties which are commercially available in the U.K.. This list changes over the years and will be different for other parts of Europe and North America.

'Conqueror' - A lovely dark red flowered variety but with the petals splashed with white at the edges. The young leaves are dark purple but change to green as they mature. This variety was developed by Latour-Marliac and has flowers up to 8 inches across when fully opened. It is perfect for a medium sized pond.

'Mrs Ricnmond' - This variety is also known as 'Fabiola' and was developed by Latour-Marliac. It has pale pink 7-inch flowers which turn red as they age. Ideal for medium sized ponds.

odorata 'Sulphurea' - This is one of the best yellows available today. It was developed by Latour-Marliac over 100 years ago and suits a small to medium sized pond. The fully opened flowers are 7 inches across but must have an open sunny site to flower really well.

'Paul Hariot' - This pink variety was developed by Latour-Marliac and is well suited to a small or medium sized pond. The flowers are 4 to 5 inches across when fully opened.

Poolside Planting

'Ray Davies' - This is basically a white variety with a lovely yellow center but the petals are also

The water lily called "Ray Davies" Photo by Dick Mills.

flushed with pink near the base. It was developed by Slocum and is ideal for a medium sized pond. The flowers are up to 7 inches in diameter when fully opened.

A pond must have some poolside planting. Photo by MP&C Piednoir Aqua Press.

There are many different plants which associate well around a pond. Many of these require moist but not waterlogged soil. These are normally found growing above the waterline next to rivers and ponds and whilst they can tolerate short periods of flooding, will die if continuously submerged. Plants such as Astilbes, Hostas, Irises and Primulas all like these conditions and in the past were used extensively in the gardens of country houses where natural rivers or ponds are commonplace.

If you have created a bog garden as part of your pond then the soil adjacent to this will tend to be moist and will probably be a good place to put these plants. If not, you are going to have to adapt your soil to suit these types of plants. Those of you with a heavy clay soil will probably have to do nothing more than dig in lots of well rotted manure to help retain moisture and make sure the plants are well watered during dry spells. For light loamy soils like mine, you will have to do more than just treat the soil if these plants are going to stand much of a chance.

Here you will have to create a reservoir of moisture under the soil by using a piece of polythene or pond liner under the plants. To do this dig out the soil to a depth of 12 inches and lay your liner in the hole. The edges should come half way up the sides of the hole. Next puncture the liner several times so that excess water will seep slowly away. Now return half the soil to the hole and mix in plenty of well rotted manure. Once the rest of the soil is returned your new moisture retentive bed is ready for planting up. During dry spells make sure this bed is kept well watered.

Whilst it is not a good idea to plant trees and shrubs directly next to a pond they can be used to good effect if planted nearby. My own pond is surrounded by shrubs and small trees on three sides to create a windbreak and provide cover for the amphibians. Among my favorite shrubs for this setting are the dogwoods of the genus *Cornus*. The spring flowering types are lovely but for all year round interest nothing can beat *C. alba* 'Elegantissima'. This shrubby plant has silver variegated leaves in the summer, brilliant autumn foliage color and spectacular red stems during the winter. These are brightest colored when the plant is cut right back in the spring and look great when seen against the

snow. Combined with *C. stolonifera* 'Flaviramea' which has bright yellow stems they create a real patch of brightness in an otherwise drab winter world.

The only trees which I would plant near a pond are miniature prostrate conifers and *Salix captea* 'Kilmarnock'. The needles shed by the prostrate conifers will fall directly under the trees and will not cause any problems while 'Kilmarnock' only grows 6 ft tall and can be netted during the autumn to prevent leaves being blown into the pond. A few will not hurt but if the whole lot end up in the pond they will rot and kill the fish.

Above: The lovely margin plant called *Hosta* "Spectacular." Photo by D. Lambert. Below: A pond can't truly be a thing of beauty without terrestrial plants adorning it. Photo by Dr. David Ford